T0149525

AND OTHER DUTIES
AS ASSIGNED

AND OTHER DUTIES AS ASSIGNED

A Fast-Track Career Guide For SUPER DUPER Administrative Professionals!

T. THEODORA BLOUNT

AND OTHER DUTIES AS ASSIGNED
A FAST-TRACK CAREER GUIDE FOR SUPER DUPER
ADMINISTRATIVE PROFESSIONALS!

iUniverse books may be ordered through booksellers or by contacting:

iUniverse
1663 Liberty Drive
Bloomington, IN 47403
www.iuniverse.com
1-800-Authors (1-800-288-4677)

Because of the dynamic nature of the Internet, any web addresses or links contained in this book may have changed since publication and may no longer be valid. The views expressed in this work are solely those of the author and do not necessarily reflect the views of the publisher, and the publisher hereby disclaims any responsibility for them.

Any people depicted in stock imagery provided by Thinkstock are models, and such images are being used for illustrative purposes only. Certain stock imagery © Thinkstock.

ISBN: 978-1-5320-3613-2 (sc)
ISBN: 978-1-5320-3614-9 (e)

Library of Congress Control Number: 2017916851

Print information available on the last page.

iUniverse rev. date: 11/21/2017

For my son, Jalen.

I HAVE MADE A CAREER out of taking care of other people. I have worked really hard, including long hours, weekends, and constant errands, to fulfill my responsibilities at work. You've never really understood what I did at work, but everything I've done in my career over the past twenty years has been all for you. You have always been my motivation to succeed, and there was absolutely nothing I wouldn't do or sacrifice for you.

It was never easy being a single parent, taking care of so many executives while you were coming home from school to an empty house and premade meals and having to manage your way through your homework. I am so very blessed that you were so smart and loving and never once got into trouble. We made it through it all, and we managed to find our quality time—even if that meant bringing you to work with me at nights while I prepared board books. We would run the empty halls, raid the vending machines, and play on the elevators.

I've had a successful career and many titles, but the one I am most proud of is being Jalen's mother.

Contents

Acknowledgments

I HAVE ALWAYS BEEN A person who loves to share ideas, skills, and best practices. I am grateful for the opportunity and platform to share this collection of personal and professional development.

First, I want to acknowledge my mother, the late Veronica Blount, and my grandfather, the late Theodore Howard, for recognizing my ability to write at such a young age. They purchased my first typewriter and pushed me to write. My grandfather never learned to read, but he wanted me to write and then read to him. I always wanted to have a new story to tell. This is the first of many books, and I promise to continue to make you both proud.

I want to thank some of the executives I had the pleasure to work alongside. These individuals helped shape me professionally:

Dr. Noel McIntosh: Thank you for giving me my first administrative role. I was proud of the work you were doing and the good it was doing for the world!

Henry Posko Jr.: Thank you for being truly amazing! I never understood what it meant to have the support of your boss in all situations until you. You gave me total control and freedom to get the job done as I saw fit. Because of that, I vowed to never let you down and to always have your back.

Cindy Plavier Truitt: Thank you for showing me what it meant to have fun at work! Your leadership style was unique and rewarding! Thanks for agreeing to wear a blue wig and parading around the halls with me. There was nothing in the world I wouldn't do for you, because you gave so much of yourself to the people.

Brad Harper: You were the first boss who made me feel like work wasn't work. I enjoyed every day working with you, and if you hadn't moved to Chicago (the coldest place in the world!), I'm sure I would still be working for you! I will always consider us the dream team!

Reneé Lewis Glover: I was so impressed and motivated by you as soon as I met you. You are one of the smartest women I know. Your heritage and love for culture are inspiring! Thank you for believing in me and giving me the power to prevail!

Alison Rand: I could never thank you enough for your astonishing belief in me. Professionally, you showed me tenacity. You are the epitome of a strong woman. You have always been a force to be reckoned with and a kick-ass girl boss! Personally, you have shown me true friendship, and your friendship means more to me than anything. I love your Jersey-girl attitude and your supersized heart! You will forever have a place in mine! I am so blessed to have you in my life as a friend and supporter. I love you!

Greg Pitts: You are one of the hardest-working men in the business! Underneath that no-nonsense exterior is a caring and compassionate man. Gaining your trust meant the world to me! I often miss your unique phrases, and I thank you for showing me persistence and what it truly means to "cook with gas."

Nicole Ashe: I may have written this book long before I met you, but it would not have reached print without your push, your motivation, and your belief in me and my dreams. You have an amazing way of inspiring people to reach their full potential, and you've served as an enormous support recognizing my abilities and talents. I am so very grateful and blessed to have you in my life.

Last, but not least, I want to acknowledge Mary Fondon. Mary, you were not the first administrative professional to report to me—and you weren't the last—but you were the one who went above and beyond anything written on a piece of paper. You truly take the phrase "and other duties as assigned" to another level! You have done more for me professionally and personally than words can explain. I love you more than you know, and I will never be able to repay you for all you've done for me.

It's Not for Everyone

ADMINISTRATIVE ASSISTANT NEEDED, EXPERIENCE REQUIRED—THINK this is you? All too often, anyone scanning job openings and reading the words *administrative assistant* assumes that it's an easy task that anyone can do. Wrong!

Not many people stood in front of their kindergarten teachers and proclaimed, "I want to be a secretary or an administrative assistant when I grow up." However, according to the US Bureau of Labor statistics from May 2016, the national estimate for office and administrative support roles is 22,026,080. If this career wasn't on the short list in grade school alongside police officer, firefighter, teacher, doctor, and nurse, why are so many people employed in this field? How did something that was once considered a job become a career?

In my trainings, I ask administrative professionals to go around the room and share what they wanted to be when they grew up, what they went to school for, and how they ended up as administrative professionals. The responses always range from astrologist to zoologist—with obstetrician and veterinarian somewhere in between. I have never come across anyone who confessed that being an administrative professional was anything more than something to start doing before pursuing another career. These people either "got stuck" doing it or—like me—discovered that they were really good at it and made a career out of it. I'm sure there are people who grew up wanting to be in this field, but it was probably more about personal passion, such as a mother or grandmother whose footsteps they wanted to follow, rather than simply an identifiable career path that would be chosen in lieu of those on the short list.

I often use the word *professional* because that's what we are. Too often, administrative professionals see themselves at the bottom of the totem pole, doing the things that no one else wants to do: filing, stapling, getting lunch, and so forth. I consider anything you've spent more than five years doing as a professional career and not a job! Working in a support role demands an extended list of requirements and know-how—some of which you may be willing to do and others they couldn't pay you enough to do. Either way, you need to know what's in store for you before you accept the job!

Look at whatever you see listed on the job description, and double it. That is the amount of work they really need done. In most cases, executives and human resources professionals who are filling positions don't know exactly what's needed to get the job done, especially if they had a good support person in the role previously. That person more than likely worked below the radar and made things seem so effortless that many of the job details went unnoticed. It was as if they magically happened.

The items highlighted on a job description, especially on the posting, are the most prevalent and visible to the job. Don't underestimate the requirements. If you really don't possess the basic skills listed, don't apply. When they include "experience with data entry and/or financial budgets," a large part of the job will probably be in data entry and/or working with financial budgets. If they list "strong calendar management" in the posting, you can likely expect at least 75 percent of the job to be calendar management. You'll be expected to come in the door knowing these things, and there will probably be little training provided.

Unless the company uses custom software that is unique to the organization, don't expect to go in and be trained in how to do your job successfully. If you are able to fly under the radar possessing fewer skills than you disclose, it won't last. This is not the secretary position of your grandmother's era. Being an administrative professional today takes more than the knowledge of how to answer telephones, transfer calls, sort mail, and file a few papers. It's evolved into a full-fledged profession that requires skills, critical thinking, and experience.

Experience over Skill

WHY IS EXPERIENCE SO IMPORTANT? Skill can't suffice on its own, because much of what we do—and do well—is because of experience. Most things we deal with on a day-to-day basis aren't things you can read about in a book. There are no books that have all the answers. There are situations when there are no written rules for how to handle them. That is where experience plays an important factor and can be a saving grace. Once you encounter something new, make a note (mental or otherwise) of how you handled it. No one's perfect, and you may not handle a new situation in the best manner the first time, especially if you are under pressure to make a decision. Keep in mind that there's no such thing as a mistake if you learn from it. If you didn't handle something as well as you would have hoped, making a note of how you could have done it better will be helpful in the future.

The more things you encounter, the wiser you become. Give yourself a few years working with different companies and for different managers—and soak it all in. Allow your brain to be a sponge. Soaking up everything will go a long way toward aiding to your success.

An experienced administrative professional has a diverse background, has worked for nonprofits and for-profits, and has worked for small and large companies. Yes, it's noble to have twenty years with the same employer, but those people—for the most part—have worked with the same people, at the same company, and doing the same things for twenty years! Companies evolve and employees can grow within the same organization, but administrative professionals need to be the innovators.

People aren't working jobs for long periods anymore. They are exploring their options and advancing their growth. This affords them opportunities to be experienced and knowledgeable in many different areas. When I review résumés for administrative positions, I don't automatically rule out those with short-lived employment stints as long as their work history is consistent and they aren't job-hopping from career to career. I've worked for three years here and three years there, and I think it's safe to say that a high-level administrative professional reaches a burnout phase somewhere between three and five years (we'll save that for another chapter).

An administrative professional with a diverse employment background can successfully adapt to a variety of situations. If you have had several employers over the past ten years, use this as a strength in your interview (as long as you were consistent in your work). If you hopped from administrative work to dog walking and then took a job as a window washer, you may need to alter your approach. You might come across as someone who is still trying to find his or her way and may appear less committed to being an administrative professional.

Employers want to know that you are comfortable and secure with performing the job at hand. Too many people use administrative work as a way in the door and want to explore other opportunities. It is not that advancement isn't a good thing, but the executive you're supporting may not be enthusiastic about giving you up after spending months or years adapting to you professionally. It is important to build a relationship with your executive and be honest about your career goals. If you're not a lifer and plan to explore other opportunities, be up front so everyone is on the same page.

Offering to train your replacement will alleviate some of the pressure of replacing you if you move to another position. A previous boss said, "Always be prepared to train your replacement. If you can't, you'll never be able to move forward."

If you're good at your job, keep all the secrets to yourself, and are afraid to show someone else how to do your job, you'll always stay in that position. Your executive will feel that no one can ever do what you do. Exhibiting strength in a position and demonstrating the ability to willingly train someone else to do your job may open you up for a promotion.

Experience may supersede skills! Today's executives tend to be more self-sufficient than the older generation of executives who could barely operate a multiline telephone system. These new age executives are computer savvy and particularly well versed in technology. Technology brings extreme benefits, but almost everyone knows their way around a smartphone and has grown accustomed to around-the-clock information via the World Wide Web.

The skills that administrative support once offered are no longer needed to the extent they once were. Not even ten years ago, as the technology curve started booming, support staff was in high demand because they needed us to show them how to work the latest and greatest gadgets. Now, even eighty-year-old grandmothers know how to send text messages! Don't be discouraged by this revelation. It's your job to stay ahead of the curve! If you have a CEO who's fascinated with technology and you need to shine, have something to teach them and wow them. This goes a long way to proving your value. If they're going 100 mph, you go 160 mph!

Always have something to bring to the table! Some executives are embarrassed when they lack knowledge in a particular area or situation, especially when others are depending on them to make decisions. You may have knowledge or information from a previous experience or job that you can share with your executive. You can also do preliminary research on the topic and present that information. Don't allow your title to limit your participation. I worked for a company that went public and formed a board. My previous experience working with boards helped me guide my executive in ways that proved to be very valuable. I also read books about how to operate a board.

If you only do as you are asked or directed—nothing more and nothing less—you are doing yourself and your employer a disservice. Your title may not include the *officer* or *vice president*, but you still have value to offer. Use your experience working for a variety of executives as leverage. You're usually the closest person to your executive, and you are in a position to offer helpful insights. Working behind the scenes often has more rewards than being in the spotlight. You don't have to take credit for the advice— the person who needs to know and understand your commitment will know.

The Interview

PLEASE DO NOT LIE ON your application or résumé. I once had a job candidate who I was excited about hiring because she listed two college degrees on her application. Only one could be confirmed, and she apparently did not tell the truth about the second degree. The administrative position for which she was being considered didn't even require a college degree, but because it was company policy that any false information result in an offer not being extended, I was not allowed to hire her.

Even if a job description states that a college degree is required, if you feel that your experience and skill set are equivalent or exceed what they need, submit your application. Employers often use the college degree to target a certain education level, but I am proof that a college degree alone does not supersede experience and skill. Always be honest.

Always dress appropriately for an interview. It is your first impression. Don't blow your chances by having a great résumé and awesome experience—and poor judgment in appearance. Most employers feel that how you dress for your interview is the most professional you will ever be. Don't make the mistake of looking up their dress code and misinterpreting how you should dress for the interview. Even if they have a casual work environment, don't go on your interview in a short skirt, jeans, or flashy club attire. Ladies should always play it safe with a pantsuit, medium heels, flats, or a skirt suit with a below-knee cut.

Ladies, do not wear low-cut blouses. This is not the movies, and your exposed cleavage might not get you the response you want. Be careful with the accessories (long, bulky jewelry and earrings) and don't wear very high-heeled shoes. Men and women need to monitor their perfume or cologne. What smells good to you may be distracting to your potential employer. You don't want them thinking they can't hire you because they don't want to smell you every day. Keep it subtle and leave the daring scent at home! Men, as tempted as you may be, don't wear khaki pants. This is a job interview and your first impression. At a minimum, wear a button-up shirt, a tie, slacks, and dress shoes. A suit jacket is suggested, but leave the sneaker-and-suit look to Justin Bieber.

Make sure your hair is groomed and your nails clean and manicured. Take extra time to make sure your shoes are polished. Avoid leaning heels and safety pins. If you can, remove any body piercings before the interview and cleverly cover any visible tattoos. If offered the position, you can always learn the company policies regarding visible tattoos and piercings before you accept the position. Never accept a position without a full disclosure if you know those things are prohibited. I'm not saying to defraud the interviewer by concealing these things. I'm just informing you that it might not be the first impression you want.

I understand that business attire can be expensive, especially if you're unemployed, but start with two versatile suits that you can interchange and possibly switch shirts and accessories. You need to keep at least two suits on hand in case you're called for a second interview. If you're called for a third interview, chances are high that you will be employed soon—so go ahead and invest in that third suit! If you have multiple interviews, try to schedule them for the same day. Scheduling your interviews on the same day will help you avoid taking off multiple days with your current employer, and it allows you to wear the same suit to both interviews.

You don't have to wear expensive clothing, but make sure it's neat and clean. Also, try to avoid walking long distances in the heat. You don't want to show up to an interview sweating or smelly. If interviewing makes you nervous, you may need to stop at a restaurant or grocery store to freshen up between interviews. I always keep an extra brush and a can of spray deodorant in the car. Do not freshen up at the place of potential employment or in your car nearby. You don't know who may see you.

Keep your cell phones and other gadgets in your vehicle. Don't even take them inside of the building. You don't want to be tempted to answer a call, and you certainly don't want to appear as if you cannot live a moment without sending a text, checking Facebook, posting on Instagram, or sending a tweet. You don't want your phone vibrating during the interview. I once interviewed a candidate, and her phone vibrated and rattled the contents of her purse the entire time. I was so distracted that I didn't really remember anything we discussed.

Any distraction can work against you. You want to keep the interviewer engaged and focused on you. I also interviewed a gentleman who entered my office with a Bluetooth in his ear. I found it distracting and odd, but it wasn't until he interrupted me midsentence to take a call that I found myself shocked. To make matters worse, his call lasted at least forty seconds, which was forty seconds of him wasting my time. Did he apologize for taking the call? Yes, but he also did not remove the Bluetooth from his ear or turn it off. Come in the door with the mind-set that you are there to give the interviewer your full, undivided attention.

As an administrative professional, I am going to hold you to a standard that I wouldn't hold many others to. For instance, it's often our responsibility to do the research, find the directions, and get our executives where they need to be on time. Therefore, do not call the employer to ask for directions while you're running late to the interview. If I am the potential employer, I am not going to hire you. If this is an example of how you're going to have me running blind to meetings, I don't need you. If you're unfamiliar with the location, use your resources: Google Maps, MapQuest, Yahoo Maps, Waze, and the like.

I often drive to the location a few days before the interview. I want to find the building and get familiar with the parking situation. Is there a garage? How far is the walk? Do I need cash to pay for parking? Where is the entrance? Even if you don't have time to go days before, leave an hour early to figure it out. Be mindful of the hiring manager's time. You certainly don't want to be late, but you don't want to be too early either. That could make them feel rushed to finish what they were doing previously and cause unnecessary stress. What you think is a good thing could throw off their schedule for the day. When you're given the information for the interview, ask if you need to come in early to complete any paperwork. It is safe to arrive fifteen minutes early. Do not arrive just in time—and certainly do not arrive a minute late.

Do your homework and research the company. Know the key players and what the company does. Show some interest. Know what you can do for the company—and be able to tell them why the company would be a good fit for you. Employers want to know that you are there for more than just money. Don't pretend that you want to work for free, but demonstrate other reasons besides salary why the job and company would be ideal for you. It could be the job location, the longevity of employment, the health benefits, or the company's mission.

Prepare a question or two that will show that you've done your homework. Asking at least one other question based on something that was mentioned in the interview will show that you're paying attention and let them know that you're interested.

A headhunter once told me to never take notes, but as an admin, I always have a pen and paper ready. If the interviewer starts rattling off names, titles, and other important information, I ask if it's okay to jot down some notes. I have never been told not to do so, and I have always used information from my notes in thank-you letters and follow-up conversations. It is impressive and important for an administrative professional to be prepared and be able to retain useful information; this demonstrates your ability to do the job.

There has only been *one* job for which I've interviewed and did not get. I was told that I was overqualified, but I believe it was because I talked too much. By nature, I am a chatty catty, but you should never talk too much to your interviewer. Don't sit there as if you have nothing to say and offer no input—and don't share every story that pops into your head. Spend most of the interview listening and answer any questions thoroughly. Use proper grammar and avoid the word *um*. If you get lost in your thought, pausing is better than saying *um*.

Speak in complete sentences and refrain from using one-word answers. Doing so could make it appear as though you're uninterested or in a hurry to end the interview.

Technology and Social Media

TECHNOLOGY AFFECTS YOUR EVERYDAY LIFE, and it will be present in your professional one as well. Some people consider the new way of communicating invasive, but it's here to stay! Before we dive into social media, let's start with text messaging. It was once a faux pas to text an employee on a personal mobile device, but it has become the norm. Texting has become prevalent in our personal lives, and it too invaded our professional lives. I have a friend whose boss texts her from the next room! It has become a common way to communicate. Some people are more attached than others, but this new way of communicating takes some getting used to if you are one who prefers good old talking!

There are many reasons why professionals text more and more frequently. Some use this form of communication as a way to multitask. They may be on a conference call on the business line, following a webinar on the laptop, and having three separate conversations via text. Others need to look busy 24-7 and text because it looks hip or gives them something to do, especially when they're in a boring meeting.

I had a boss who would text me at one o'clock in the morning to determine if I was awake and available to take a call. People see texting as a noninvasive way to contact you, leaving you with the ability to choose to respond or not—especially at one o'clock in the morning! What do you think happens if you respond to a text from your boss at one o'clock in the morning? Your boss will believe it's okay to call or text more crap at one o'clock in the morning next time. Would that drive you crazy? If so, you need to establish some boundaries. I ignored the one o'clock in the morning text message, and I addressed the issue the minute I arrived at work the next morning. There's a way to professionally address any situation. Even if you have agreed to be on call in your current role, there should still be parameters around exactly what that entails.

I once read an article that warned professionals about using text lingo in professional arenas (LOL, IDK, etc.). Now there's literally no getting around it. The cooler it becomes, the more it happens. My sixty-year-old godmother uses text lingo at every opportunity she gets. It's like she's waiting by her phone for you to say something that allows her to respond with LOL, TTYL, IDK. I'm not going to offer any suggestions other than to remember what's professional and unprofessional. There's a line that can easily be crossed in this arena. Be careful.

I didn't use some of the more common text lingo that can be a bit suggestive. You don't have to spell out the word to be offensive. I sat across the hall from a chief external affairs officer who called me into his office to decode lingo that was sent to him by a colleague. He was stunned to learn what it meant. Text messages can easily give you a false sense of security. Before you know it, you could be communicating with a colleague on another level. Text messages can always be saved and traced—be careful!

I've run into a few situations where employees wanted to be reimbursed for minutes used or overages caused by exceeding their text messages and/or minutes with their cellular providers. Not everyone has unlimited service, and even if they did, employers must be careful when expecting employees to use their own personal devices for work. If you are concerned about the use of your personal device, have a conversation with your employer. Don't let a $500 bill pop up in your mailbox and put on the verge of going postal before you have the discussion. Your employer may offer to provide an office-issued device.

Many employers are dishing out company-issued devices because they want to make sure you have all of your emails at your fingertips at all times. Make certain that you understand the expectations of having a company phone. I once had a manager complain to me that his assistant didn't respond to emails in a timely manner. After inquiring, I learned that he meant emails sent after hours. Since he provided a company phone, he expected the employee to respond to every email. You need to have a clear and concise discussion about your employer's expectations and acknowledge what you're willing to provide.

There's no such thing as a true nine-to-five admin professional, but if you know you have after-work limitations, you must address it before it becomes an issue. Don't set a standard that you aren't willing to or simply cannot maintain. Don't be the employee who always responds to every email even from the dinner table until your spouse and family has a problem. Once you stop after you've created a standard you can't maintain, it may be considered a setback.

My mother always said, "Don't start what you can't finish."

You want to be accommodating, especially when starting a new job, but don't give what you don't have. Otherwise, you will end up bitter. If you set your expectations early, everyone will know what to expect. Also, keep in mind that *everything* done on a company-issued mobile device (phone, iPad, laptop, etc.) is the property of said company. Don't get carried away and start using the device as your own personal device. That is not a good idea. Every email, picture, and text can be stored and viewed by the company.

When you sign off on the company's computer/mobile device usage policy, know that they will likely uphold every right they have—and then some. Also, your company may be subject to an open records request at some point, which means the company may not be the only ones seeing your information. Those who submit an open records request (usually with good cause) could gain access to your data. Don't send pictures you don't want anyone and everyone to see and be mindful of your emails and instant messages. I know someone who was terminated over an instant message where he said something about another employee. The company was able to go back through months of instant messages to retrieve a history. Don't let that happen to you.

Social media is a popular way to stay connected with old friends, schoolmates, coworkers, and neighbors. For the most part, it can be a fun way to update your friends and loved ones about what's going on with you, but be aware of what it can do to you professionally.

There are hundreds of news stories about social media in the workplace. Teachers are told to unfriend their students, and employers are monitoring their employees. You must be mindful of what you say, do, and post. Be mindful of who you link with, friend, tweet. More companies than you can imagine are using social media to research potential candidates. Everything you say—and every picture or video you post—will be on the World Wide Web forever even if you remove it from your site. Once something goes viral, you have no control over it. Think three times before you hit the send, upload, post, or tweet button.

Did you know that associating with a disgruntled employee could keep you from getting a job? If Jane Doe leaves ABC Company on really bad terms, you might not know everything she's done. You might not even know her that well. Maybe she's never even mentioned ABC Company to you. However, if she's on your LinkedIn account or your Facebook page, and her former supervisor—who considers her *big* trouble—searches your profile and learns you're connected with Jane, your potential employer will not call you to ask about your association with Jane. The supervisor might not bring you in for an interview if Jane is the type of company you keep. No laws would have been broken. There's no discrimination case to be filed because you were never even called for the job. You would have no idea why you weren't selected. You may have no knowledge that they've even seen your online profile.

For the most part, most employers have no issue with social media. In fact, businesses are being encouraged to enhance and increase their online presences. Social media outlets have proven to be very successful tools for many businesses. However, even with the acceptance of social media, most companies restrict the use of these media outlets in the workplace. Make sure you are aware of your company's policy.

Be mindful of what you have on display and how that information can be used to judge your character. Do you have teenage children who are linked to your social media accounts? Does your son have a photo of himself posing with a BB gun in your living room? How does your boss know this is a BB gun? What is he or she thinking of you as a parent? Does it matter? It could. Maybe he or she lost a relative to gun violence, and this is a sad reminder of that incident. Maybe this will have him or her questioning your judgment. If you've said something unpleasant about a former employer, it may still be out there. One of your friends may repost it when you announce your new gig. Be careful and very mindful.

Some photos can be detrimental to your career. The little things you overlook may come back to haunt you. What happens if you call in sick—and then one of your friends posts pictures of you at the beach with the girls? Don't post photos of yourself drinking with the guys or your trip to Vegas with the girls. You do not need your boss or coworkers seeing those photos. Know your job, your position, your boss, and your potential customers. If you support an advertising executive whose next big client is an advocate for animal rights, you don't want to be on a social media outlet wearing your fur coat at a company holiday party.

Video chatting can be an awesome job perk, but the opportunity to telecommute and work from home or another remote location can lead to problems. If you're conducting business, it is not okay to wear pajamas as you Skype or video chat. It is not okay to wear anything that would be deemed inappropriate in the workplace (tight-fitting clothing, low-cut blouses, offensive T-shirts, etc.). It is not professional to have an abundance of background activity (music, children running around, dogs barking, etc.). Don't allow the comfort of your own home to create an awkward environment for others.

It may seem like there's no privacy anymore and that you have to be worried about everything, but—no matter how careful you may be— things can happen. Keep your personal accounts personal and create professional accounts to network. Some of you are smart enough to block all of your information so only "friends" can see it. Good for you—but what happens when you start friending coworkers? Everything you say and do has a chance to make its way back to the office.

As an administrative professional, be cautious about who you allow into your social circle. People's perceptions are their realities, and if you hold a high-level, confidential position, you may want to have as few coworkers in your social circle as possible (if any). If I am the executive assistant to the CEO and have twenty coworkers on my Facebook page, it may be perceived that those twenty people out of three hundred are in the know—and that I share all the company's secrets with them.

Be careful with social media. If it becomes more trouble than it's worth, pull the plug!

The Professional Marriage

FOR ALL INTENTS AND PURPOSES, the relationships we share with our immediate supervisors are more like professional marriages! So much of what we do is about the relationship. We have a relationship with someone we might not even *want* to know if not for the job. These professional marriages require just as much effort as real marriages—if not more. At least with your real spouse, you love him or her enough (hopefully) to want it to work. You may or may not be willing to give it your all to make it work with your supervisor.

In a real marriage, there's an equal balance of give and take. Professionally, it is up to us, the administrative support, to learn about our supervisors and adapt to them. You cannot say, "I know he's this way, but I'm going to change that!"

Many people think that way about their real spouses. They marry someone and hope for the chance to change those one or two things that they know they could change—If only their spouse would listen!

The person you sign on to support will still be that same person in five years. There are some things that can change for the better once you show him or her that there are other ways of doing certain things. You may be able to convince your boss to start using a car service to and from the airport instead of having you or someone else in the office drive. Depending upon how much the car service charges, it may cost less and cut down on your mileage reimbursement, the salary spent for you to play taxi, and the time you spend away from work. Even if he's "been that way for years," it may be one of those rare instances where you can alter that behavior. That is more of an exception to the rule than the rule. You can also change things for the worse. You can start a job and spoil your supervisor so much that he or she expects more than what is reasonable.

What happens if your supervisor comes onboard after you? What if you are in the position before a new manager is hired? Please don't think that this gives you liberty to "school" your new supervisor on how things are done, should be done, or were done by your previous supervisor. That is a no-no! It is your responsibility to accept your new supervisor as an individual and learn his or her personality and work style. It is important to understand and accept your new boss despite whatever commitment or bond you shared with your previous boss and despite the circumstances of your previous boss's departure. You wouldn't want your spouse telling you everything that his or her previous spouse/girlfriend/boyfriend did better than you.

Your new supervisor must feel that you are genuinely dedicated to him or her. If you can prove your loyalty, you will make yourself invaluable. Your new supervisor will have someone to rely on to bring him or her up to speed and help with the learning curve while absorbing the new place and new people. You must be someone your new supervisor can trust!

Many executives prefer to hire their own administrative support and not use the ones in place because of a lack of loyalty or trust. You can prove that you're an asset by making it your objective to adjust. That is where your relationships within the organization can help or hurt you. If your overall approval rating is high among your colleagues, managers, and security guards, word will travel to your new boss. He or she may consider you an attribute based on the perceptions of others and the professional relationships you have groomed. It is important to build and maintain professional relationships with everyone. You never know if or when others will have a say in your fate.

The best thing you can do is learn everything you can about your supervisor. Don't be nosey or get yourself intertwined in their business and personal matters. Learn their pet peeves, their likes and dislikes, and their moods and signals. Getting to a point where you can foresee their next step before it happens will keep you ahead in the race. You should be able to successfully predict what will set them off. If you're a super-duper admin, you will predict those things and find ways to avoid them—or at least soften the blow.

If you know that your boss is not usually a happy camper after board meetings, avoid scheduling anything on their calendar on the day of the board meeting. Don't schedule anything before the board meeting because your boss will be too focused on predicting the outcome and will not be able to focus on anyone or anything else, which may prove to be a recipe for disaster. Save yourself, your boss, and other people.

Don't schedule meetings directly after the board meeting either because if the board meeting goes well, the accountant they're interviewing immediately after the board meeting may be hired because they're in a good mood. What if it's the other way around? What if the board meeting didn't go well? What then? Don't put your boss, yourself, or innocent bystanders in the path of destruction. Be a super-duper admin, use your telepathic powers and clear their schedule for the day. If your boss continues to put other meetings on board meeting days, kindly suggest that it may be best to leave that day open in case there are unexpected things that need to be done in preparation for the meeting or after the meeting. Bosses may schedule meetings for those days and not understand what they're doing. It is our job to know what they need even when they don't.

I doubt that many married people have full access to their spouses' email. Even if you do have access (maybe you share a home computer), I doubt that you open, read, and reply to their personal emails on a daily basis. Many administrative professionals have access to their executives' emails because it's our job to scan them, respond to them, prioritize them, and maybe print them. I've always asked my executives to let people know that I have access to their emails because I never want to be tempted to read something about me. It is awkward to see an email from their spouse when the subject line reads: "I'm sick of this S#@!"

I had a boss whose wife knew I read his emails, and she also knew that I didn't open the emails from her. She occasionally would write explicit or angry subject lines. If I had an inkling that they had a bad night or morning at home, I would leap from my desk and make sure everything was how it was supposed to be—or better—to reduce the chances of him ruining my day.

When he walked into the office without poking his head into my office to say good morning, my suspicions were confirmed. I would listen carefully and calculate each step and every move. Ten minutes with no words meant I had done my job. I would even head people off at the pass if I knew they were headed to his office with stuff he didn't need to hear. I was like a six-foot-four, three hundred-pound linebacker tackling people as they approached the three-yard line (the threshold of his doorway).

I don't know if he ever realized that the days when things weren't going so swell at home were the days that things were just peachy at work.

Then again, he was a very smart man. Maybe he and his wife duped me and put on the façade of an unhappy home so that I would guarantee a stress-free day! I need to call him when I'm done writing this book to get the answer to that!

Stay in Your Lane

IN SOME CASES, ADMINISTRATIVE PROFESSIONALS are given levels of authority that, if they are not careful, they can unintentionally abuse. Yes, we all know someone (maybe even when we look in the mirror) who intentionally abuses this level of authority, but for the sake of trying to give people the benefit of the doubt, let's stick with *unintentionally*.

You must learn to stay in your lane. Refrain from becoming the despot of your department! You will be given a certain level of authority and the right to make decisions on behalf of your executive. Some people will be intimidated by this, but if you abuse your superpower, you will lose the respect of those around you and alienate your executive.

You never want to come across as a bully who abuses that superpower. You can get people to follow you faster with respect and admiration than with fear and intimidation. Fear and intimidation may get people to do what you ask them to do, but they won't respect you—and they won't be loyal to you. If you come across as someone who bullies your way into situations, especially those that are really of no concern to you, you will gain a team of people who will await your demise. Before you know it, people will only include you in the things where there's an opportunity to use you to get what they want. For example, if they need a bully, they bring you in, sit back, and let you be the bully. They get to walk away and keep their hands clean. Be careful if you think people always go to you because you know how to get the tough things done. If they do, there's probably a reason for it.

Just because your executive allows you to make certain decisions and gives you a level of authority that exceeds your job description, don't think you can assume the responsibility of his or her role. Some administrative professionals forget their true roles and begin offering suggestions and opinions. They insert themselves into anything and everything, and their suggestions suddenly become soft demands. Many of these department despots don't realize that they are despots because the executives (even though they are aware of the problem) are often too apprehensive to address the issue. They may choose to ignore the issue or determine that they are able to use this character trait to their benefit.

Even if your immediate supervisor has not addressed the issue, take heed of the signs around you. Do you come across as bossy? Do people push back when you're giving your opinions? Most of us welcome the suggestions and opinions of those around us, unless they are always offering their opinions—even when not asked and especially if they come across as someone who wants to force their insights down your throat.

Don't be tempted to feel that it is your right to know the everyday dealings of your executive. Some people get so consumed with their executives' lives that they become controlling and demanding. If your executive is on a telephone conversation or has someone in the office and the conversation turns confidential or you can hear them lower their voices, get up and gently pull the door closed to offer them privacy. Even if they did not close the door, you should make the gesture to assure them that you always have their best interests in mind. Don't assume that you are privy to any information because your boss didn't close the door.

Never repeat or question your boss about any conversation when he or she was not directly speaking to you. If you overhear a conversation that was not intended for you, don't approach your boss with thoughts or suggestions. Allow your boss to come to you. The same applies to email conversations.

Lose any sense of entitlement, stay in your lane, and embrace your role. My past executives respected the fact that they could give me authority and feel confident that I wouldn't abuse it.

The Nonvacationing Boss

VACATIONS ARE NOT JUST FOR the supervisor because the rest of the staff also benefits when the boss goes on a vacation! Unfortunately, the supervisors who need to take vacations the most are usually the ones who don't. Administrative professionals are more likely to experience burnout faster if they have supervisors who do not utilize their vacation time. You can use all of your own vacation time, but unless your supervisor also takes time off, you don't reach your full rest potential. It's not like we're not busy when the boss is off. In many cases, we're even busier when they're gone. We can only hope that they're not one of those supervisors who physically go on vacation but keep in touch all day via emails, text messages, Skype, faxes, Pony Express, and so forth.

There are a number of reasons why leaders don't take time off from work. Some truly don't have faith in the people they leave behind to actually be able to function in their absence. These supervisors need to question their own hiring judgment because you shouldn't have people in roles who you don't think can actually do the job.

Other supervisors live and breathe the job and simply can't stop working—even if they tried. I feel sorry for them because, in most cases, they place the job before family. If they refuse to take time off or don't fully commit themselves to their families when they are off, they usually end up alienating their families.

Some supervisors need to feel important around their families and friends and constantly check in with the office to boost their own importance and relevance.

This is not a complete list of why supervisors don't take vacations, but the stress level in the office is certainly intensified when the boss is always there. I often utilized time when my boss was away to get organized and caught up on outstanding items. That was in the few instances when the boss wasn't calling to check in every hour on the hour.

What can you do? There's probably little you can do to alter your boss's behavior, but you can find creative ways to cope. Don't always take your

spouse in on the hassles of work and give your best friend an earful of the unpleasantness at home.

I started using my travel time for music and reflection. Sometimes I listen to gospel music and let myself settle into a calm, reflective space. Sometimes I listen to music that makes me cry, and sometimes I listen to old school music that allows me to reminisce about when I was younger and worried less. When I worked a job in the city and had a very long commute, I especially dreaded Monday mornings. On Sunday evenings, I would download new music to my phone for my morning commute. I would use the Shazam app throughout the week to create a list of songs I liked. I would even use the app to capture songs I heard in dressing rooms and restaurants. I looked forward to my new playlist on Monday mornings, and it helped me transition from weekend life to workday life.

You need to be mindful of the same baggage from home. Life happens, and we can't count how many mornings we've had to juggle a thousand things before we even get to work. Leave that life suitcase and its baggage at home. That may sound easier said than done. There are times when we must bring some of our home baggage with us. If the kids missed the school bus, you may have to turn around and go get them or make calls to find someone else who can. If you have car trouble and have to drop off your car on your way to work, that means that personal baggage is joining you for your ride.

How do you make certain you leave that suitcase in the car if makes its way into the parking lot with you? You do your best to resolve what you can before you go into work, and when you get into work, you refrain from unleashing your home life onto your coworkers—even if they are people you confide in and consider friends. When we unload our stress onto others, it changes the mood and the environment, and we relive it all.

I'm not saying that you can't be personable with your coworkers, but refrain from oversharing and becoming so casual with your coworkers that they start to view you and your personal life as a distraction.

It is a best practice to at least not share as soon as you get to work since your emotions may be raw. Your coworkers likely have their own issues and circumstances to deal with before work. I worked in an open-office space with several other administrative professionals on an executive floor on multiple occasions, and there were always people who came to work every day and talked to every coworker about their family drama from the weekend and had personal and very loud phone conversations about that drama. I know these people understood that their conversations could be heard, but they were so engulfed in themselves and their situations that they never considered anyone else. To make matters worse, the executives rarely addressed the behavior. They preferred to close their doors rather than manage that problem.

There are other times when work and life intersect, and it isn't bad. People at the office may inquire about family vacation or trip. If we get a promotion at work or are working on a big project, we often share the news with family. A popular phrase is *work-life balance,* and the key word is *balance.* You must be able to successfully balance the two, and awareness is the first step to managing this!

Burnout / Planning Your Exit Strategy

I HAVE AN UNDOCUMENTED THEORY on the burnout time frame for high-level administrative professionals. I believe that those of us in certain roles reach our burnout potential in three years. The first year is spent getting to know your new supervisor, the job, the place, and the people. By year two, you kind of know what you're dealing with. Even if you're no longer ecstatic about the position, year two flies by. By year three, you may be starting to wear down. Some people find other positions within the company, some begin to slack off from the excellent job they were doing in year one, which results in mediocre performance, and others leave.

Year one is the honeymoon. In year two, you know exactly what you've gotten yourself into. If you can survive year three, you're home free until you get to year five. The fifth year is the last testing moment. In some companies, you're not fully invested until year five, and some people use that as an incentive to hang in there. By year five, you have pretty much come to grips with who you are, what you do, and who your supervisor is. If you make it to year six, then year ten is a stone's throw away. It is smooth sailing after that.

For the record, I will fully disclose that I am not a lifer. For the most part, I have a three- or four-year track record. I used to find this was a setback, but it's difficult to gain a certain level of experience from working at one job for ten or twenty years. It's not that I don't find this to be a loyal, devoted, and committed act. I have always looked for opportunities where I thought I could be in it for the long haul. I admire people who can say, "I've been here for twenty years. I remember when we had shag carpet and John Robertson wasn't a vice president. He was a security guard, and Kyle Platt had an Afro bigger than the world globe in Gloria Leopard's office!"

Those stories had me longing for an opportunity to be in that position, but I'm always going 150 mph and on to the next best thing before my seat gets too warm. If I find myself losing interest in a position, I reinvent it. In many of my jobs, I started doing one thing with certain responsibilities, and usually just a few months in, I evolved into another position—and doing about twenty other things. In some cases, my title changed, and in other cases, it did not. In some cases, my salary changed, and in other cases, it did not. I always have to be busy and stay challenged. Otherwise, I will fall into the category of workers who come to work every day and do the same mundane work with little to no effort and little to no enthusiasm or drive.

I'm not suggesting that the way I have chosen to move about my career path is fitting for anyone else, but you should enjoy what you do, appreciate what you do, and have something to offer. If and when you feel yourself slipping into a serious funk, maybe you need to plan your exit strategy.

In our positions, we sit alongside some of the most influential people in our organizations. We mirror our supervisors, and in many ways, people monitor our behavior as true signs of the state of the agency. We must be careful about how we're perceived. If there are twenty-six administrative professionals within your organization and you support the president and CEO, you'd better believe that everyone is evaluating your performance as it compares to the others'. After all, the president and CEO should have the best of the best on their sides. You don't want to slip into a place where your funk alters who you are as a professional. Don't go to a place where you're no longer at the top of your game because you've become so fed up that you no longer desire to be the best.

In one of my positions, my predecessor became so overwhelmed and stressed in the role as the senior executive assistant to the president and CEO that she demoted herself and took a lower-level, lower-paying position in another division of the company. She, unfortunately, allowed the position to get the best of her. Ultimately, even those within her new department began to judge her ability to function under high levels of stress. She was eventually dubbed "the one who had a breakdown," and her adeptness within that company was forever questioned. I don't know all the logistics of what occurred prior to my arrival on the scene, but she seemed like a very nice, proficient individual. Maybe she didn't have the gusto to continue at the rate in which our supervisor required.

In another position, the person who sat in the chair before me had started out to be extremely operative, and from what I hear, she was bright; however, she'd allowed the stress of the position to get the best of her, and she began slacking off, allowing her in-the-funk days to outweigh the good ones. Apparently, she just started showing up to work—nothing more and nothing less. Ultimately, she was asked to move on.

You never want to be asked to leave. It usually takes a supervisor, especially one in a high-level role, a lot to make that move. CEOs want to minimize turnover in their administrative professionals because high turnover can reflect poorly on them—no matter the reason for the turnover. I know CEOs who brag about how long they've had their admins in comparison to their counterparts. Everyone's watching, including their families. By the time you're asked to leave, you more than likely should have walked away six months before or sooner.

Don't pretend that the problems don't exist, and whatever you do, don't allow your professionalism to change because you're in a bad situation. My professional reputation means more to me than any situation I've been in. I've worked too hard to build it up for it to be tarnished by a series of events at one place of employment. When I look for my next job, I want my previous supervisor to have nothing but great things to say about me.

I make sure I leave before I allow things to get too bad, and I leave while I'm still on top. Leaving on your own when they were just as ready for you to go is just as bad as being asked to leave. Executives tend to keep their assistants from twelve to sixteen months after they've decided that they want to end the relationship. Many executives are afraid of that period between the current support person and the next one. It's difficult to start the hiring process without the current person knowing. Many executives are concerned about the amount of time it takes a new person to learn and adapt. Often executives feel that it's easier to keep someone they don't really want rather than starting the process again.

Telltale signs that it's time to go:

- if you start having daydreams or out-of-body experiences that you are slapping your boss repeatedly and his or her head is bobbing like a doll glued to the dashboard of your car
- if you need to bang your toe against the corner of your desk to keep from yelling, "Shut the hay up!" while your boss is telling you something for the third time that day

- when you start reserving a middle seat for his flights, pretending that nothing else is available, and knowing that he absolutely despises sitting there
- when you dress up at Halloween as your boss and your costume accessories include a pointed hat, crooked teeth, and a broom

All kidding aside, you will know when it's time to go. I will caution you to leave on the best terms possible, which means no gossiping about your boss to others and no being rebellious. Whatever you do, don't stop giving it your all. Give 110 percent until your very last day! You want to leave when you're on top, and you don't want to burn any bridges on your way out.

If you were feeling underappreciated, what better way to leave than on a high note? If you offered things they didn't recognize, they will often notice them when you're gone. You wanted them to recognize your worth while you were there, but that doesn't always happen. Just think of it as paying it forward. If an administrative professional wasn't appreciated until after he or she departed, maybe the next one will be appreciated more. If this pay-it-forward cycle continues, eventually you will land in a role where it finally benefits you!

I was a part of a management training session where the HR supervisor told us that we were implementing a new system. She was new to the company, and this new system was probably one of three we'd tried in the past six months. Needless to say, no one was thrilled. She basically told a group of managers, attorneys, vice presidents, and senior vice presidents that working for the organization was a privilege and a choice. We were not slaves, and no one was making us stay there. If we had problems with the way things were being done, we should leave because there were plenty of people—some with PhDs—who would love to have our jobs.

That statement reinforced that I no longer wanted to work there. However, as unprofessional as the statement was, it caused me great reflection. It was sad—but true—that none of us had to stay there.

I often teach administrative professionals to plan their exit strategies because nothing concerns me more than having a bunch of unhappy people in the workplace. No one wants people dragging in and out, barely doing their jobs, and leaving more work for others. That sort of behavior, if tolerated, causes low employee morale. While I don't agree with the method in which the message was delivered, if you chose to come to work every day, you must do what's expected of you and nothing less. Even if you feel like your employer is unworthy of your 110 percent, give it to them anyway. In the end, you will know that you didn't allow their shortcomings or misguidance to change who you are as a professional.

Unhappy? Unappreciated? Underutilized? Plan your exit strategy. It's simple. Once you decide that you're in a place where you no longer wish to be, it is your responsibility to alter the outcome. Planning an exit strategy works differently for everyone. Some people may have a two- week plan, and others may have a one-year plan. Make sure your plan is conducive for you and continue to give your all until the very last day.

Don't Save the Worst for Last—Do the Worst When You Are at Your Best

THERE WILL BE THINGS YOU like to do in this role, and there will be things that you won't like to do. Whatever the reason for your dislike of a particular task—it's boring, mediocre, not your job, or you're not good at it—the worst thing you can do is tackle the task when you're anywhere but at your peak. If you are a morning person, your peak is early morning. That is when you're the happiest or most energetic. You should schedule your most difficult tasks or those you dislike for the mornings. If you are not a morning person, the last thing you want to do is take on a task when you are at your lowest, most unenergetic time of the day. It's like adding insult to injury. If you generally get sleepy after lunch, avoid after-lunch meetings or schedule your days accordingly.

No one knows you better than you. It's important to evaluate yourself and learn your strengths and weaknesses. You don't have to broadcast your weaknesses, but you should know them. We all have weaknesses, and the best way to conquer them is to know what they are and learn ways to manage or maneuver around them. You may be tested in an interview. A potential employer may ask you if you know your weaknesses or ask you to name an area where you need work. Don't make the mistake of stating that you do not have any areas of improvement. We all do. It is important to know your weaknesses or areas of improvement for your own professional development. Being aware of this area and having a solution or method of improvement will demonstrate that you are aware that you're not perfect and that you're committed to professional development.

If you're not the fastest typist, try reading the document first to get an understanding of what you're typing so you can type at a faster speed. If you have difficulty remembering things, get in the habit of writing everything down. It will become second nature and help you significantly. If you despise math and are not a morning person, plan to complete your balance sheets toward the end of the day (when you're at your peak).

Know your weakness and identify your peak times of the day and week. Learn the office pattern and know which days are the busiest and which are the least hectic. Save your most challenging tasks for the quiet days. That way, you're not trying to focus on a difficult task and juggle a busy office at the same time. Complete your easy tasks or things you do very well on hectic days. If you plan accordingly, you should be able to manage the chaos of ringing phones and the revolving door of visitors and still get a fair amount of work done. You won't always be able to predict how your days will go, but you should have a pretty good idea of the usual pace of the office.

At one company, Fridays were the busiest days because most people did things at the last minute and crammed a week's worth of work into one day so the reports would be complete by their due date on Monday morning. It was not an ideal way to work, but if you know how others around you operate, you can prepare yourself by completing your more difficult tasks during the beginning or middle of the week and are prepared for the Friday rush. At another company, Fridays were the easiest because the executives had worked hard all week. By two o'clock on Friday afternoon, they had wrapped things up and were headed for their lake houses with their families or the golf course with their friends.

The secret to being a super-duper admin is making things look effortless and almost coming across as if there's nothing you can't do well. You and I know it's because you have strategically planned to do the harder things when you have more time to function and the easier things when your attention will be demanded elsewhere, but that's our little secret!

Measuring Your Success: Pay Increases and Performance Reviews

IN MANY OF MY TRAINING sessions and one-on-one consultations, people often say, "I am not appreciated. My boss does not thank me. He doesn't value my contribution. I don't think my performance appraisals accurately reflect the work I've done."

Unfortunately, those of us in support roles are often recognized for the things we don't do more often than we are for the things we do. I don't believe this is solely because we're not appreciated. The magnitude of what we do is so wide, and there are so many moving parts that we're habitually going a hundred miles per hour. Many of our tasks fly below the radar.

If you are responsible for opening the office—turning on the lights, starting the coffeepot, opening the blinds, watering the plants, and bringing in the newspaper—would you want your supervisor to walk in every morning and say, "Thank you for turning on the lights, getting the coffee ready, opening the blinds, watering the plants, and bringing in the morning paper"? Some people may say, "Yes—and I want them to acknowledge that I was there on time too!" If that is your stance, that job is most likely not the best for you.

You can schedule more than one hundred meetings a year, but unfortunately, the one conference call you forget to send out the dial-in information for or the one conference room you failed to reserve will be remembered and noticed—even if the other ninety-nine go smoothly. It is not that no one noticed how the other ninety-nine went well—they were supposed to go smoothly—but it's your job. That is what's expected. The one that didn't go well—where something went wrong—stood out from the rest and will get some attention. Don't be discouraged. It's the same thing with the newspaper delivery. The paperboy delivers the paper every morning. That is his job. You only notice the morning that he doesn't deliver it. It is the same thing with scheduling the hundred meetings.

If you're in finance, it's easy to track your success. If you stay in the black, you're doing well because it's in black and white (and not red).

You're successful at what you do. Your boss can see your progress by simply pulling a budget report. If you're in human resources, if you're attracting great people and your retention efforts are working, you're doing well. If you're in the legal department and winning cases or avoiding lawsuits, then you're doing well.

As an administrative professional, a variety of tasks determine your success. It is your responsibility to measure it. You can gauge your progress/success and make sure your supervisor is aware of your progress and accomplishments, especially if your supervisor does not provide professional feedback.

I worked for one CEO for three years, and I received no written form of professional feedback. While there was the occasional "good job" and a few spot bonuses that translated to "good job," there was never a meeting to discuss the things I was doing well and the things I could have done better. I hope that all of us in this profession desire to be the best we can be and welcome the opportunity to learn about the areas we can improve.

I will be the first to tell you to keep a log! The log will help with performance reviews, and it's an efficient tool for documenting your progress. Give yourself a high five! Log your accomplishments, things you did well, and tasks you completed. Log any new processes that you initiated or improved. Your log should include dates so you can refer to them accordingly. When you're ready to ask for a raise, it would be beneficial to showcase your accomplishments throughout a period that exceeds one calendar year.

You can also use your log to help you write your accomplishment statement on your résumé or cover letters. I often boast about the fact that I helped an organization save $500,000 on office supply spending within my first month of employment. Make sure your current employer knows this information, and it's great information to share with potential employers. Everything you do well at your current job will prepare you for your next job, and everything you don't do well at your current job should serve as a lesson about what to improve at your next job.

It's okay not to know everything. A mentor or sponsor can help you understand the company and the way it does business, which will help you understand your job better. Once you learn how business is done and understand the different components, you will be able to work faster. You will understand different acronyms and have a better understanding of key players and job functions. It's much easier to assist a caller when you know who is responsible for what. It's much easier to read your boss's illegible notes when you have an idea about the context.

In addition to keeping a log, you should set professional goals. Most companies set goals for the company and/or individual departments. In addition to these goals, you should set goals based on your own desires and the goals of the department. One of my personal goals deals with successful organization.

How do you measure how successful you are within organization? How long does it take you to locate something you've filed? I set my own target of two minutes or less to find anything: a hard-copy file, an electronic file, a book, magazine article, or anything else. When my supervisor asks me for something, the clock begins in my head. It's a race against time to see how fast I can get it back to him or her. When I can turn it around in less than a minute, that's a success for me!

Whether my supervisor notices how speedy I can retrieve things or not is okay because the goal is for me. Consistency in this area builds confidence in your abilities. At some point, your supervisor will realize that you are extremely organized. You'll probably learn if your supervisor is paying attention to how fast you respond the first time it takes you five or ten minutes to get something. Your supervisor may say, "What happened? Can't you find it?" That is a sign that your supervisor noticed when you returned quickly—even if there was not any verbal acknowledgment of your speed. You're setting a standard, and it's a great idea to set standards, but keep in mind that the standards you set can also be your downfall if you're not willing to uphold them.

Set goals and acknowledge your own accomplishments so you can give yourself a pat on the back if you need one. For example, everything we do during a day can be reason for personal celebration or a reward. If you are ordering lunch for eight vice presidents, you know that there will always be a few lunch divas in the crowd. The lunch divas—male or female— will never be satisfied with their lunch orders. You watch these people in action and wonder what it must be like for their spouses and friends to sit through dinner with them at a restaurant. If they act that way at a table full of colleagues and complain about a free lunch, what are they like when they're among family and paying for their meals?

You can use these situations as accomplishments. VP 1 orders her salad with extra onions but absolutely no olives. She wants to substitute the house dressing for balsamic vinaigrette. VP 2 wants extra olives and wants to substitute the balsamic vinaigrette that comes with his salad for the honey mustard that they usually only serve with chicken tenders. VP 3 doesn't want croutons, tomatoes, carrots, or anything else that comes on the salad with the exception of lettuce and cucumbers. This lunch order is complex because, no matter which restaurant you order from, the chefs apparently cannot bring themselves to dismantle their precious salad creations and remove everything that makes a salad great to dwindle it down to simple lettuce and cucumbers. You almost have to get on the phone with the chef and say, "I know how crazy this sounds, but please no shredded cabbage, no sprinkles of feta … nothing … nothing on this salad but lettuce and cucumbers, no dressing, no croutons, no pepper, just lettuce and cucumbers please!"

You can forget it if you must type all the special orders into an online system that allows a maximum of twenty characters for comments! You may have one who only drinks a special brand of water, one who refuses to drink from Styrofoam cups, and one who will only drink water at room temperature. If the office is cold, you must set a bottle of water on the windowsill an hour before the meeting so the sunlight can bring it to the right temperature.

Even something as effortless as ordering lunch for eight people can turn into an event. You place the lunch orders in front of them, personally survey the orders, and confirm that the orders are correct. In many cases, you correct them yourself. You ask, "Is everything okay? Does everyone have what they need?"

They are too busy chopping away at their lunches to answer. When you witness the nods of approval, you gently close the conference room door behind you and dance down the hall to your desk. That is an accomplishment. It is a small one in the grand scheme of things, but it is an accomplishment all the same.

When you foresee these challenges, enter the task with a game plan. When you know the unique requests, learn how to handle them in a way that does not add stress for you. I had to build relationships with the various restaurants so they understood the diverse requests. If I only had cold food orders, I ordered the food far enough in advance so we had time to run back out before the meeting to correct the order if necessary. When the meetings included more than ten people, I took away the option to order as individuals and ordered a variety of salads and sandwiches.

I learned what the majority preferred to eat. With the exception of my special salad guy, it was fairly easy to place orders for the group. By setting the standard that any meeting that exceeded ten people in attendance would warrant a group order, I eliminated the chaos and the stress of increasing the percentage of lunch divas.

When the lunches were held three times a week, I had to have a plan to make sure they were executed without a hitch. I cleverly dwindled down to once-a-week lunch meetings because the meetings sometimes became consumed with lunch, and it really distracted from the real course of business. I approached my supervisor, the CEO, and didn't make it about me having difficulty with the lunch orders. I approached it from the standpoint of meeting effectiveness and time management. We rescheduled two of the weekly meetings to take place before or after the lunch hour, which eliminated lunch. We improved the effectiveness of the meetings, and it helped me with my issue as part-time waiter and psychologist.

When you successfully order lunch and they all have what they ordered, that's an accomplishment. Give yourself a high five, do a dance, or reward yourself with a piece of chocolate if you need a constant incentive. Use every opportunity to measure your progress and determine areas for improvement. If you're setting up a conference call, your goal should be to have the call set up on time, make sure the connection is clear, and confirm that everyone expected to participate on the call has the correct dial-in information. Foresee any potential problems so you can correct them before someone asks you to.

If you have three conference calls per week, your goal should be for all three to go off without a hitch. If something unforeseeable happens during one of the calls, review what went wrong and brainstorm ways to prevent it the next time. We once had a caller who was supposed to be on another call accidentally dial in on our call because, like most offices, we used the same dial-in information repeatedly. This individual had participated on a call with our company the day before and inadvertently dialed into our conference line when he was attempting to dial into another company's line. Apparently, he jotted down our dial-in information instead of the other company's information.

Since the conference call was discussing our budget and financial information and we now had a third-party vendor on the call, I knew my supervisor would not be pleased. Therefore, by the time the meeting ended, I had already contacted our conference call service provider and researched our options for more secure calling. We immediately upgraded our plan to one that allowed us to provide our own custom security codes for each call. Being able to provide custom security codes would prevent anyone not intended for the call to participate. The initial problem occurred, but I found an immediate solution. You will not be able to foresee every problem, but when you encounter a new one, work on a resolution. The ability to solve problems will be one of your finest assets.

For the most part, employees resent performance appraisals. Unfortunately, many managers use that time to tell their employees all the things that are wrong. There really should be no surprises in a performance appraisal. Effective managers provide constructive feedback throughout the year, usually on a case-by-case basis. That eliminates any questions about meeting the supervisor's expectations.

A performance appraisal should be a time to review your progress. If there was an issue, you should be reviewing your progress and improvement since the onset of said issue. If you don't have a supervisor who provides ongoing feedback, maybe you need to set up monthly or quarterly meetings and ask for the top three things you're doing well and the top three things you could do better. Don't be afraid to ask about areas for improvement. That is the only way we can enhance our professional growth.

Managers often dread performance appraisals because when the appraisal is not 100 percent in the employee's favor, employees tend to take it personally and alter their behavior afterward. Keep an open mind—and don't take what you're being told personally. You have to take personal responsibility, but don't associate the negative things your supervisor says about your work as an indicator of how he or she feels about you personally.

I've had more than one person work for me who I liked personally, but I didn't necessarily find their work to be outstanding. If you create a situation where your behavior changes or you contradict everything being shared with you, you run the risk of having a supervisor who feels that you can't handle constructive criticism. Your supervisor may become unwilling to approach you, which may result in you being terminated because the things you don't do well will go unaddressed. It may get to the point where the only solution is to remove you.

If your unwillingness to receive constructive feedback results in you being terminated, is it worth it? It's not okay for a supervisor to terminate you solely because he or she couldn't manage you because you were unresponsive to performance appraisals. Your supervisor should be able to address any areas of improvement—whether you are responsive or not. If you're not responsive and don't correct the issue, you should be disciplined—even if it means termination.

The problem with constructive feedback is that many employees don't appreciate the way it's delivered. Some of the employees I have coached spoke of instances where a correction took place in front of others. Some employees didn't like the supervisor's tone or felt that they were only disciplined when the supervisor was in a bad mood. Setting up frequent feedback sessions will eliminate the bad timing of occasional feedback. Make sure your feedback sessions occur often enough that current issues can be addressed in a timely manner. I suggest daily or weekly touch-base sessions or one-on-one meetings with your supervisor to review the calendar, address any outstanding items for which you need input, and take a minute or two to address any concerns.

Initiate feedback for recent meetings and other projects for which you've been tasked. If you ask for feedback, it's likely you will get immediate, honest feedback while it's still fresh on your supervisor's mind. Seeking this information will afford you the ability to correct any mishaps sooner than later. Maybe you hosted an executive meeting and thought the worst thing that happened was lunch was delivered late. The executives didn't give a second thought about the food, but they were concerned that the overhead projection was too dark, the temperature was too warm, and no one knew how to operate the thermostat. That gives some insight that you may have not received if too much time had passed. With this knowledge, you can immediately have someone replace the projector bulb in the conference room and ask someone from building services to show you how to properly operate the thermostat. You can ask if the temperature is satisfactory at the beginning of future meetings and adjust as needed.

How do you get your point across during a performance appraisal? In some cases, employers ask employees to complete self-assessments. If you have the ability to do this, your log will prove to be beneficial. Officially document your accomplishments, and be sure to include instances where you were given a two-week deadline and completed the project in half the time. You don't have to list everything. Stick to items that make the most impact and keep a running list of your smaller accomplishments to use during the dialogue. If your company or supervisor does not ask for self-assessments, approach your supervisor beforehand and get permission to submit a self-assessment.

You don't want to blindside your supervisor and submit it during your performance appraisal. In many cases, your supervisor may not have time to read it. Your supervisor could feel like you are bombarding him or her. If he or she is aware that you want to submit a self-assessment, you can submit it in advance of your appraisal. You especially want your supervisor to see your self-assessment before your appraisal if the appraisal is tied to performance compensation. You want your supervisor to be reminded of your accomplishments before a final decision about your compensation is made. The things you've tracked in your log will often be more extensive than what your supervisor can recall.

You can never measure where you've been and what you've accomplished if you don't keep track of things. Don't assume that you will be able to remember everything. Your log should be just as much for you and your personal growth as it is to help during your performance review or job search. In this profession, it can be to gauge success. You should take personal responsibility of this.

It is extremely important to welcome, accept, and acknowledge constructive criticism and feedback. We all are who we're perceived to be. You alone cannot determine if you're a good employee, parent, neighbor, or friend. If asked the question, we would all say that we're good at these things, but the reality is that we're probably the only ones who don't get to determine those things. Your supervisor and colleagues determine if you're a good employee. Your spouse, children, and family determine if you're a good parent. You can believe that you're the best neighbor ever, but if

75 percent of the people in your neighborhood don't care for you, you're probably not a good neighbor.

We need feedback in every situation to get better in what we do. If you ask your teenager if you're a good parent, depending on his or her mood, that answer may not be accurate. For the most part, those around us know us best. They see what we can't see. Embrace the feedback that you receive and use it for growth.

We all want to be paid more. No matter how much money you make, you're going to want more. You often feel that you deserve more. Aside from merit increases that are associated with performance reviews, when should you look for a pay increase? This is always the most pressing topic of discussion in my focus groups. You should never ask for a pay increase without substantial cause. Just because you take on one minor responsibility or task doesn't mean you should go asking for more money.

If you consistently take on additional tasks, it's okay to document the tasks and their frequency and write a proposal for your supervisor that explains the added tasks and mentions a potential pay increase, bonus, or promotion if warranted. Be careful. You can't go looking for a raise or promotion for every little thing you do that's considered above and beyond your job.

No one wants to work without being compensated accordingly, and I'm not suggesting that you do. Don't sell yourself short because you deserve to be paid what you're worth, but be careful about demanding more money every time you're asked to do something.

Being able to show the value you bring to the company and the money you save will go a long way in pleading your case for a raise.

And Other Duties as Assigned

I HAVE YET TO FIND a job description that does not include the words "and other duties as assigned." What does this really mean? Your employer may or may not know all that your job entails. That clause allows an employer to simply include anything that comes up. An experienced administrative professional would never work within the confines of a job description. Don't fall into that trap.

I teach my trainees not to say, "That's not in my job description." Those words should never be more than a thought that remains in your head. Those of us in support roles often find ourselves taking on more and more tasks every day. The better you are with things, the more responsibility you will undertake. However, don't think of this as a negative thing. It's a positive thing, and I can teach you how to use it to your benefit.

The phrase "it's not my job" will certainly come back to haunt you. It may even make your supervisor feel like you're not a team player. I often wonder if the phrase "and other duties as assigned" was invented by a ticked-off employer who threw it in when an employee said, "That's not in my job description." Maybe the person writing the job description couldn't think of any more little things and decided to write "and other duties as assigned" to make sure he or she didn't leave anything out. Even if your job description doesn't have those five words, pretend that it does. Don't do only what's asked of you. Do the things that aren't asked but you know should be done. That trait separates the beginners from the professionals. That is a quality of a great administrative professional—not those who are just good at what they do.

You won't always be recognized for going that extra mile, but persistency and consistency will pave the way. You will be recognized at some point. I talk to my teenage son and say, "If you're the floor sweeper, be the best floor sweeper you can be. Even if you sweep floors for an entire year and no one ever mentions the wonderful job you've done, you will know that you gave it your best. If they didn't recognize it while you were there, they will recognize it when you're gone."

An administrative professional who takes charge and has a get-'er-done attitude will continue to press forward. That person is a super-duper admin!

How to Be a Super-Duper Admin

LEAVE YOUR EMOTIONS OUT OF your job! The first thing you want to do is learn not to take everything personally. The executives you support have difficult jobs and are often burdened with numerous responsibilities. They will not always be able to convey messages to you in the most pleasant way. There are times when they need to be firm and direct with you to convey the urgency of a situation. Do your best to gauge the situation/mood and know how to adjust accordingly. If you and your executive share lighthearted conversations and humor, know when it's not appropriate. Your ability to successfully acclimate to your executive's mood and the situation at hand will work in your favor and make you stand out from the rest.

Always be professional! In many cases, we are the closest people to our executives. If we're truly super-duper admins, we become their confidants and people with whom they can let their hair down behind closed doors. We will learn a lot about our executive's personal and business lives. We must remain professional at all times. No matter how friendly you become with your exec, always give him or her the respect the position deserves. No one outside of the two of you needs to know how close the two of you are or how friendly you've become. You don't want others to have the perception that you can only work for this one individual and that you wouldn't be successful working for anyone else because your alliance is with one person.

In addition, being too relaxed with your exec in the company of others may be perceived as a lack of professional respect for that person, which could ultimately damage your professional reputation. Always position yourself in a professional manner with all employees regardless of your personal/friendly relationship. Know what to wear and what not to wear to work. Even though some things may not be addressed with you directly, it doesn't mean you should wear them. Many supervisors are reluctant to address dress code infractions because they generally result in difficult discussions. There was once a woman who wore a baseball cap to work every day in a corporate office setting. Even if the dress code is business casual, it doesn't mean coming to work looking like you're ready to spend a day in the park. Be professional.

Be mindful of how much personal information you share and how often. Parents returning from maternity leave often overshare photos of their new babies. Your newborn is very exciting to you, your family, and most of your coworkers; however, after a few days of sharing new photos every day, it can become a nuisance. Some will deem it as unprofessional if it distracts others from their work.

Keep personal telephone calls to a minimum. Even if you have your own office, limit your personal calls. Your family should only call you at work for urgent or important matters. People who are frequently on personal calls appear as though they don't have enough work to do. If you sit in an open area or cubicle and must make a personal call, use an empty conference room or utilize your break time to go to a more secluded area or your car. Your coworkers and visitors don't need to hear your personal conversations with your children, doctors, babysitters, parents, siblings, and spouses.

I once worked with several other administrative professionals in an executive office with an open floor plan. The personal conversations were very distracting; the executives would often get up from their desks and close their doors to avoid the loud conversations. Executives need to take responsibility and clearly communicate their expectations, but any true professional should understand how to be appropriate and not place executives in that position.

Confidentiality Is a Must!

Unless you are a news anchor on the six o'clock news, you're not in the business of sharing the daily news. The biggest mistake you can make is confiding in other people about what's going on at the top. You will be privy to more information than some of the other senior-level executives. If you support the president and CEO, you will likely know more than everyone because not all senior-level executives will know it all. If you support the CFO, you will likely know the true financial state of the business and not just what they tell everyone. If you support the CHRO, you will likely know more than others in terms of salaries, bonuses, terminations, inappropriate conduct, and investigations. No matter what area you support, you must understand the importance of confidentiality and understand how it directly aligns with your reputation and character.

People should not feel comfortable asking you anything they wouldn't ask your boss. People have stopped speaking to me because I refused to share information. I don't need to lie and say I don't know. I'm comfortable with telling them that if it were meant for them to know, they would know. We are privy to information sooner than others, and sometimes the others are never told. You can't take it upon yourself to determine what people should and should not know.

If a major crime or law is not being broken, keep your mouth closed. You should report crimes, but things are not always fair at the top. Some people will make more money, some will get higher bonuses, and some will be fired with or without good cause. You won't agree with every decision, but you need to stay in your lane. Be careful not to project your personal opinions—and refrain from being the one with loose lips.

Most executives rank trust and confidentiality at the top of their lists. If you can demonstrate a strong work ethic, trust, and confidentiality, you will be an asset to your boss and the company. If you waver from this, they likely won't want you around too long. They will see you as a liability—and you will be just that.

Be Your Own Cheerleader

We are often recognized for the things we don't do more than the things we do. We are not going to be thanked for everything we do—not even the big things. Our jobs are to make things go smoothly, and we are simply doing our jobs when we achieve that. Find ways to reward yourself for your accomplishments. You can use a daily to-do list with checkboxes for completed items. Each time you check one of the boxes, you should take pride in that, especially if there are many days when you can barely get through your email. You can get creative and use different colored pens or markers. You can write the more difficult tasks or urgent tasks in red. I often use what I call the traffic-light system (red light, yellow light, green light) for much of my work. I will use a red highlighter for very important items that are not completed, yellow for items that are in progress, and green for items that are completed or need no further action.

The more visual you make your tasks, the more visible your progress will be. Even though it may be small, it's still motivating as you celebrate your accomplishments. If you love Post-It notes, you can use the same traffic-light system with the colored or neon-colored notes. My workspace is often full of Post-It notes. I will jot down a task on a Post-It note and stick it to my computer monitor or dry-erase board. After I complete a task, I enjoy snatching the Post-It note and throwing it in the trash.

It's rewarding to start the day with several Post-It notes and then dwindle them down to one or two. You can also distribute the Post-It notes to others. If I write down "return Jane Doe's call" and a coworker is the best person to assist Ms. Doe, I can hand him or her the Post-It note with Ms. Doe's contact information.

If you try to avoid sweets or coffee, use those as incentives. I have a large bowl of chocolates on my desk. If I tell myself I'm not going to have a Reese's unless I knock out all the yellow Post-It notes or if there are no complaints from the executive meeting, I reward myself when I've accomplished those things. No matter how you decide to define your personal reward, make it simple. Use something that will remind you of your progress throughout the day. Don't set unrealistic expectations for yourself. You know your typical workday, and if you're like me, there's never a day where you can get it all done.

Be Organized

The best thing you can do is prioritize. You may be given a hundred things to do in a day, fifty of which are high-priority tasks, and have two hundred emails, forty-five phone calls, thirty instant messages, and twenty-five people dropping by your desk for help at the last minute.

I once told a supervisor that if he made everything a priority, nothing would be a priority. It is impossible to work in the red all day with everything you're given being a top priority. You must be able to prioritize each task—with no two tasks being of equal priority. Complete one task before you move to the next. Ideally, you will complete the most important items of the day.

If you assist your exec with email, you can use the traffic-light system to create subfolders or custom flags. Use red for important emails, green for emails that are not urgent but require a response or decision, and yellow for emails that are just for informational purposes. That system will allow you and your exec to be organized, and it will save time.

You can also adapt a color system for the calendar by color-coding the calendar notices accordingly (red for a meeting that cannot be moved, yellow for a reoccurring meeting with internal attendees, green for blocked-off personal-planning time, blue for external meetings, orange for committee or outside board meetings, and so on). Color-coding meeting notices will help you and your exec stay organized, and it will help when multiple people support an exec or when you're out of the office and need someone to support your exec in your absence.

Set up meeting spaces at least fifteen minutes before meetings, making certain the conference call dial-in is working and ready, the audio-visual equipment is working properly, and all documents, food, and beverages are prepared. You never want the leaders to walk into a room and tell you what to do. You should know the space very well and not need step-by-step guidance for every detail. Once you prove that you're organized and gain their trust, the meetings will go smoothly. They will entrust you with every detail and leave you alone so you can execute. You will be able to focus on the task at hand without several people barking orders at the last minute and throwing you off your schedule.

Don't Be a Know-It-All

Don't be afraid to admit that you don't know everything. Learn how to ask for help. Be open to seeking out a more experienced admin to serve as your mentor—one you can learn from. Be willing to share your knowledge and skills with your peers. If you can foster supportive relationships with your fellow admins, you will become an asset to the team and the company.

Whatever you do, don't try to make yourself look good by making others look bad. We have all encountered someone who was a know-it-all. That person enjoys humiliating people by knowing everything. We don't know everything, and you don't want the one time you're wrong to be the highlight of someone's day.

Embrace your knowledge. You don't have to dummy yourself down for anyone. Just be mindful of others. You want people to have your back and not be ready to stab you in it the first time you make a mistake. It's all in the way you present information. You can be the most knowledgeable person who everyone wants to come to for information because you know how to deliver it in a way that doesn't belittle them—or you can be the most knowledgeable person who no one wants to ask anything because you make them feel stupid for not knowing.

There will come a time when you drop the ball and need one of your fellow admins or someone else on your team to bail you out. You don't want them to not help just because they want to see you suffer.

Own Up to Your Mistakes

I have no patience for people who make excuses and can't admit their mistakes. Don't waste time trying to prove to your boss why you were right or make excuses for why something didn't happen.

I admit fault and apologize before I'm even sure if whatever took place was truly my fault. I would rather admit fault and find out later that it wasn't my fault. You are human and are going to make mistakes. The worst thing you can do is fail to admit when you've made a mistake or minimize a situation to save face.

Sharpen Your Skills

The worst thing you can do is limit yourself to the same work routine every day. Sit in on meetings with your supervisor to learn more about what's going on with the company. Work in dual-computer environments (PC and Mac). The more knowledgeable you are about computers and software, the more of an asset you become. I work in a PC environment at work and in a Mac environment at home. I often take time to teach myself new ways to do things within programs. If you ever wonder what an application does or what happens when you do this or that, spend some time pushing the buttons, visiting each drop-down tab, and exploring the functions.

Shortcuts are your friend. The day you can show your boss how to use a shortcut is the day you prove that you know how to be efficient with your work. You don't always have to take classes and attend workshops to sharpen your skills. Take the opportunity to learn what's around you. Do you know that taking the time to read the company newsletter when no one else in your department reads it makes you valuable? Just knowing about a planned fire drill can make you look like a rock star when you place a reminder on your exec's calendar and purposely schedule his or her morning meetings around the drill.

YouTube is your friend! You can YouTube or Google just about anything. I always say, "I'm smart, but I'm not that smart. If I can think of something, someone probably already invented it." If I think there must be a way to make a process easier, it's likely already been created. Nine times out of ten, it has already been created!

You can study something as simple as the phonetic alphabet. This will make booking flights and many other things easier since you will be able to correctly recite confirmation numbers and email addresses. It's a small thing to learn—and it's almost like another language—but it will make you appear more professional.

Learn everything you can about smartphones and the newest gadgets and apps. Having technology-related knowledge and experience is a plus and will always come in handy. Learn about all the audiovisual equipment in your building, especially in the areas you use. Learn how to operate the equipment so you can eliminate the need to call someone from IT every time there's an issue.

Your ability to resolve issues on the spot will not go unnoticed. They may not recognize it when you do it, but when you're off for the day and they must fend for themselves, they will recognize your value.

Build Relationships

In our field, it is important to build relationships. Admin professionals often don't realize the need for networking and building relationships. If you don't have business cards, make sure you have some made right away. If you already have business cards, don't keep them locked in the desk drawer and only give them to vendors. It's important to network and build relationships with others within your company and outside your company.

Building relationships can help your boss as well. Say you attend a company-sponsored event and are sitting at a table with the HR director of a huge power company, and your company plans to host a fundraiser—and that power company is on the short list of potential companies to approach for a donation. If you and the HR director exchange information, maybe she could be your inside contact or put you in contact with the right person.

I've always established great working relationships with the administrative support that supports my executive's colleagues. On many occasions, I could call one of the other admins (even from outside companies) and have them work in my favor to get a meeting scheduled or canceled at the last minute.

If you don't build relationships with these people, why would they want to help you? You would be no different from anyone else—and your requests could go unanswered. People tend to help people they know and feel comfortable with. Don't alienate yourself from others.

Challenge Yourself and Add Value

No one knows you better than you do! You know your heart, and you know what you want even if you can't always convey it. If the job becomes meaningless and you run out of ways to challenge yourself, you need to plan your exit strategy. What we do can easily be considered mundane if you allow it to be. Stay engaged and challenge yourself frequently. If you're thinking, *But I don't want to challenge myself; I just want to go to work and collect a paycheck*, it's likely that you are already showing up in a less desirable way to your boss and coworkers.

You can't smell your own perfume or cologne because you get used to it over time. That is the same thing that happens when you don't challenge yourself to be better. That is what happens when you just show up at work and do not engage or perform. You don't see it because you've become accustomed to it, but those around you see it. Even if it seems like no one has an issue because no one has addressed it, they're taking notes. They likely want you to be gone just as much as you want to go.

I do not enjoy the same work routine every day. I find ways to challenge myself. I take on tasks that I don't know very well to keep me involved. I volunteer for things that are out of my realm just for the exposure to something new. You should never settle for the same old, same old, because it will get boring—and you will begin to hate your job.

You must always find a way to add value. I have a friend who's been laid off from almost every job he's had. No matter the financial state of a company, they will rarely let go of their top talent. If you have set yourself among the best of the best—even if they can no longer afford you—they will find a way to keep you in some capacity. It may mean letting go of two people to keep you or asking you to take on more duties or a smaller role.

Even if the added value is small, it's better than adding no value and making yourself easily dispensable. I've been in the room when leaders were forecasting head count reductions, and while they do consider salaries and the overall dollars they need to save, they often look at the people who are more valuable to the company. It is not contingent on title. They may need to cut a VP role to save money, but they'll opt to cut two senior managers because the VP has offered more.

Define Your Own Success

You should never measure your success based on someone else's. You must define what makes you successful and that's not always a job title or salary. Even if you did not inspire to be in a support role, you must make the best of where you are. Discover what makes you passionate. Turn your passions into goals and use your goals as stepping stones to create better opportunities. Do not sit and wait for opportunities, you must go after what you want. Ambition and determination alone won't make you successful. It takes more than feelings and wanting to do something to achieve success. When you define your own success, and set your own path to achieve that success, the personal reward and self-achievement will far outweigh anything noticeable to the naked eye. Success is not always what you see; it's often how we feel. Do not compete with others, compete to be your very best. When you are the best that you can be, and give the best that you have to offer, you are successful!

About the Author

THE AUTHOR SERVED FOR MORE than twenty years as an administrative professional for presidents and C-level executives for private, publicly traded, and nonprofit organizations. She's held nearly every support title in the field, including administrative assistant, executive assistant, senior executive assistant, administrative lead, administrative manager, office manager, and administration manager.

She has mentored, trained, and managed administrative professionals at all levels. She was once responsible for the hiring of all support staff within an organization, training them, and creating company-wide policies and procedures that helped them be successful in their day-to-day roles. Her leadership roles have afforded her the opportunity to provide job leveling in organizations where the titles and salaries weren't consistent among support staff.

The author has also provided management training and served as a liaison between support staff and senior management. She's conducted numerous team-building activities, off-site engagements, and retreats for support staff and C-level executives.

This book provides insights into support roles and their daily functions. The book is intended for those currently in support roles and those considering careers in support roles.